Mother and Child
(Rabbit and Lamb)
2004
Bronze, black patina
86.5 x 37 x 29.5 cm
Courtesy Mary Boone
Gallery (New York)

Reclining Figure (Lamb)
2004
Bronze, black patina
44.5 x 69 x 45 cm
Courtesy Mary Boone
Gallery (New York)

Torso (Lamb)
2003
Bronze, black patina
86 x 38 x 32 cm
Courtesy Mary Boone
Gallery (New York)

Torso (Ewe)
2004
Bronze, black patina
93 x 29.5 x 59.5 cm
Courtesy Mary Boone
Gallery (New York)

Reclining Figure (Venison)
2004
Bronze, black patina
44 x 113.5 x 60 cm
Courtesy Mary Boone
Gallery (New York)

Standing Figure (Beef)
2004
Bronze, black patina
154.5 x 47 x 54.5 cm
Courtesy Mary Boone
Gallery (New York)

Torso (Stag)
2004
Bronze, black patina
131.5 x 57.5 x 54 cm
Courtesy Mary Boone
Gallery (New York)

Seated Figure (Bull)
2004
Bronze, black patina
179.5 x 93 x 87.5 cm
Courtesy Mary Boone
Gallery (New York)

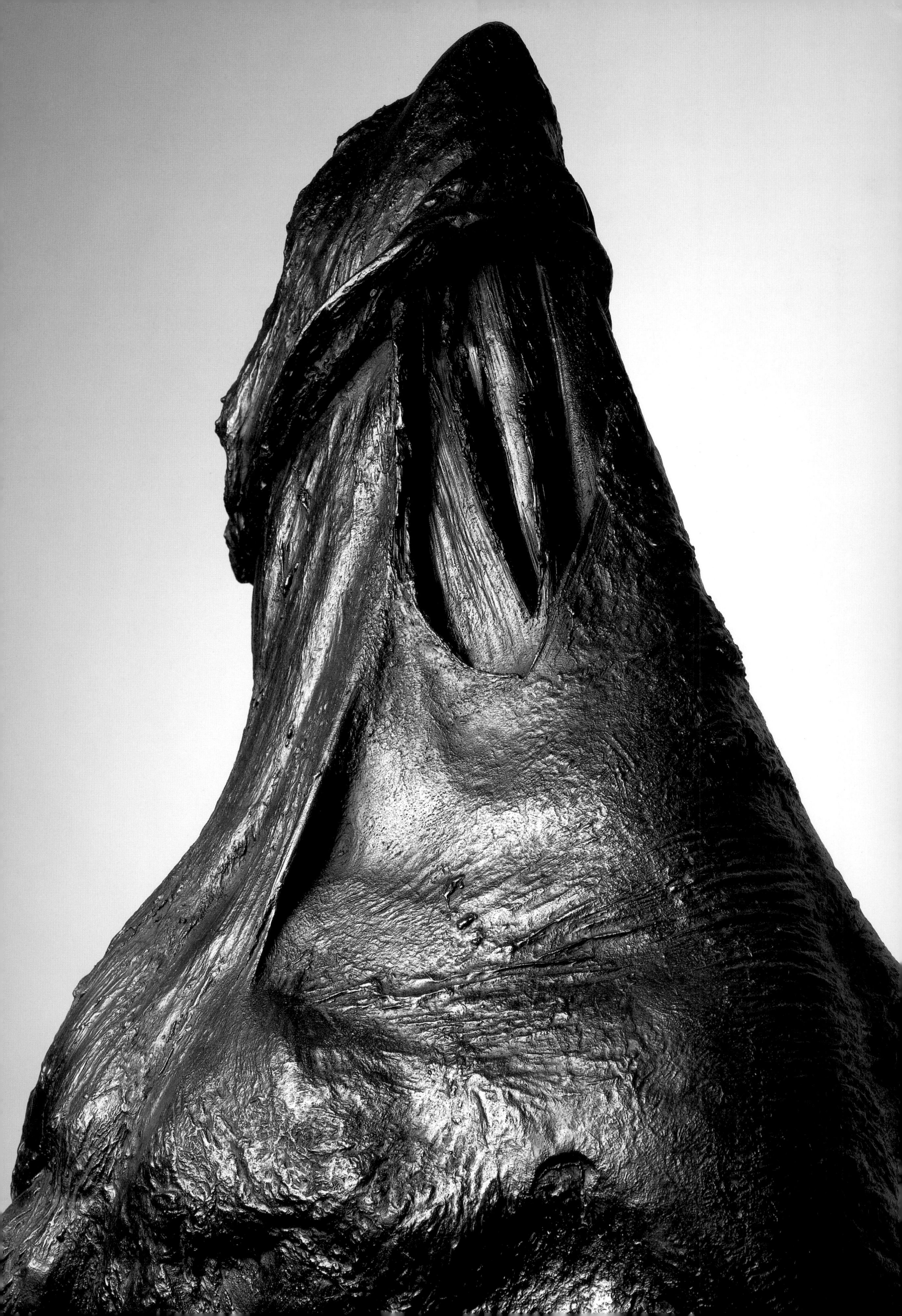

Seated Figure (Bull)
2004
Bronze, black patina
179.5 x 93 x 87.5 cm
Courtesy Mary Boone
Gallery (New York)

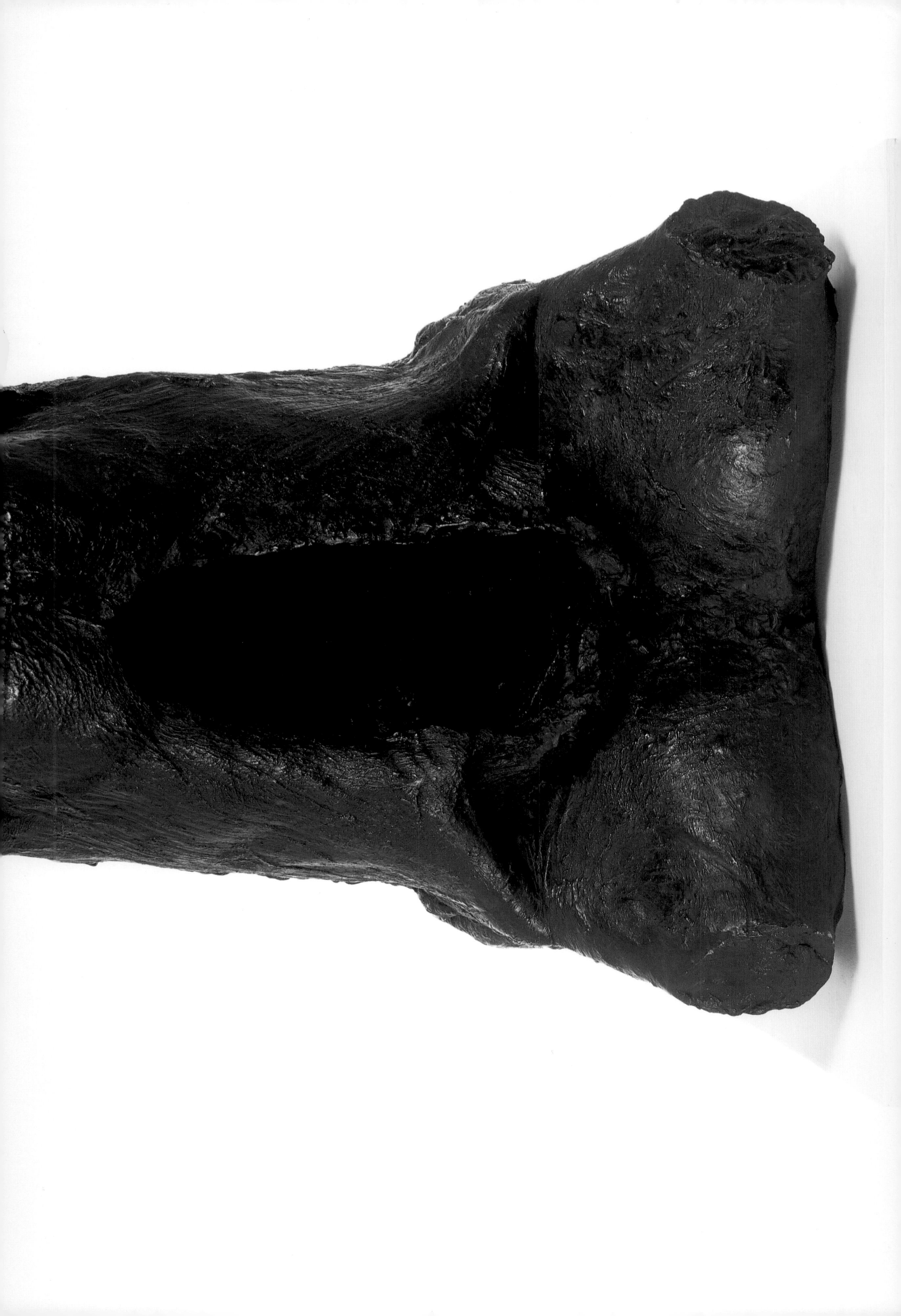

Standing Figure (Rabbit)
2003
Bronze, black patina
33.5 x 16.5 x 14.5 cm
Courtesy Jay Jopling/
White Cube (London)

On Its Elbow (Rabbit)
2004
Bronze, black patina
14 x 33 x 16 cm
Courtesy Jay Jopling/
White Cube (London)

On Its Elbow (Rabbit)
2004
Bronze, black patina
14 x 33 x 16 cm
Courtesy Jay Jopling/
White Cube (London)

Reclining Figure (Rabbit)
2004
Bronze, black patina
13.5 x 34 x 17 cm
Courtesy Jay Jopling/
White Cube (London)

Cross-legged Figure
(Rabbit)
2004
Bronze, black patina
13 x 39 x 16 cm
Courtesy Jay Jopling/
White Cube (London)

Lounging Figure (Rabbit)
2004
Bronze, black patina
15 x 41.5 x 22.5 cm
Courtesy Jay Jopling/
White Cube (London)

Lounging Figure (Rabbit)
2004
Bronze, black patina
15 x 41.5 x 22.5 cm
Courtesy Jay Jopling/
White Cube (London)

Right-handed Figure (Rabbit)
2004
Bronze, black patina
38 x 20 x 10 cm
Courtesy Jay Jopling/ White Cube (London)

Klystron d'un système radar
(années 1950)

dur de PC

Antenne satellite (1992)

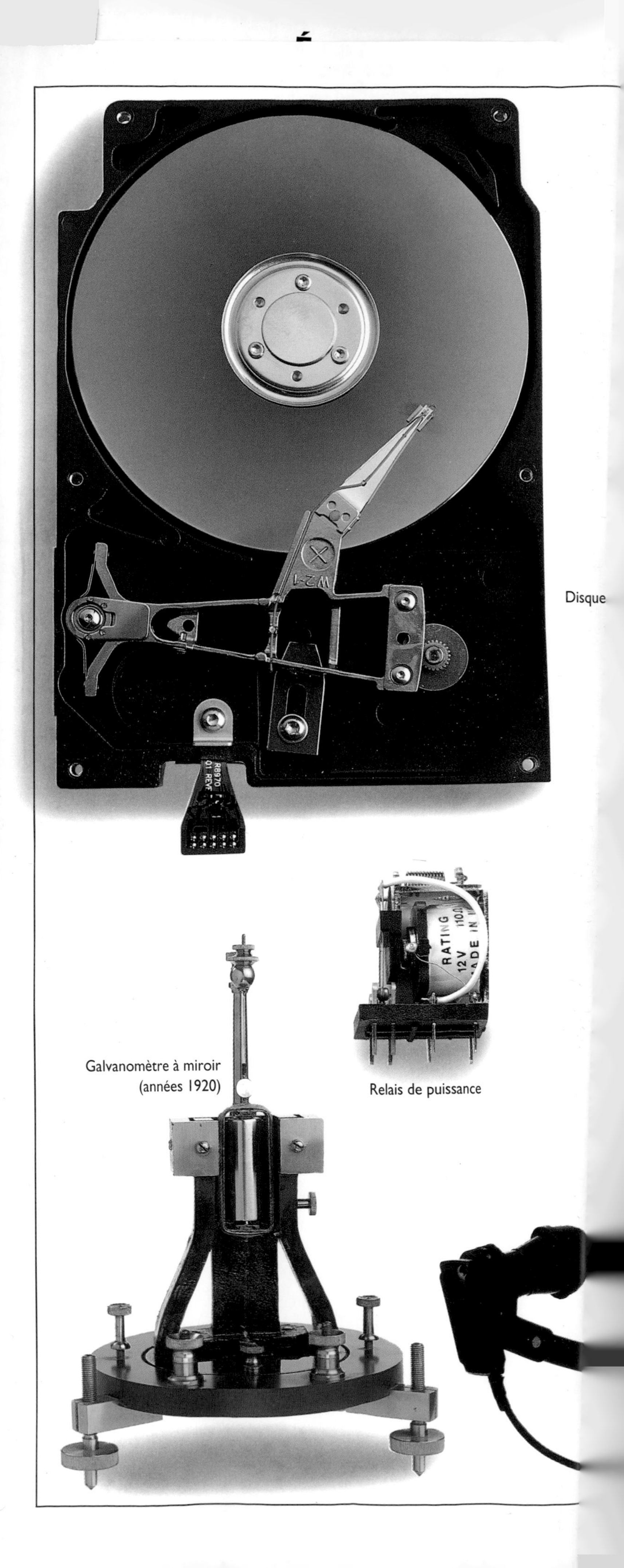

Disque

Relais de puissance

Galvanomètre à miroir
(années 1920)